C000091929

WIRRAL
THEN & NOW

IN COLOUR

DANIEL K. LONGMAN

COLOUR PHOTOGRAPHY BY BARNEY FINLAYSON

The
History
Press

Dedicated to
Ian & Marilyn Boumphrey

First published 2011
Reprinted 2013
This edition printed 2015

The History Press
The Mill, Brimscombe Port
Stroud, Gloucestershire, GL5 2QG
www.thehistorypress.co.uk

British Library Cataloguing in Publication Data.
A catalogue record for this book is available from the British Library.

ISBN 978 0 7509 6373 2

Typesetting and origination by The History Press
Printed in China

CONTENTS

ACKNOWLEDGEMENTS

With thanks to:

Barney Finlayson
Emily Found
Namfon Day
Dave Matthew Karellen
John Seddon
Alex Evans

ABOUT THE AUTHORS

Daniel K. Longman

Birkenhead-born Dan is the author of many local history books: *Criminal Wirral*, *Wirral Tragic Tales*, *Criminal Liverpool*, *Criminal Wirral II*, *Liverpool Then & Now*, *Merseyside War Years Then & Now* and *Not a Guide to Wirral*. He specialises in researching the darker side of Merseyside's long and fascinating past, and holds a particular interest in the region's historic criminal underworld.

Barney Finlayson

Barney Finlayson is a full time GP based in Prescot. He has a genuine love for photography and has travelled the world to capture some truly impressive scenes. From golden dawns amongst the vast green landscapes of Scotland to stunning panoramic vistas amidst the bustling cityscapes of New York, Barney has managed to document a remarkable array of pictures in his own unique style. (www.barneyfinlayson.com)

INTRODUCTION

Wirral is a small peninsula situated in the northwest of England, sitting between the River Dee and the River Mersey, with a coastline washed by the Irish Sea. It contains numerous little neighbourhoods, such as Tranmere, New Brighton, Bebington and many more besides. They all contribute to Wirral's vibrant social history, which dates back many years; evidence suggests that habitation upon this 'myrtle corner' was from as early as 7000 BC. Through the centuries, Wirral has been home to the Celtics, Romans and Anglo-Saxons, not to mention the settlements of the Vikings and the Normans. These lands have been a distinctive, war-torn melting-pot; a bloody rainbow of cultures and nationalities, all of which have shaped this unique area into the Wirral we know today.

Of course, all of this rich and wonderful history is mainly shrouded in the shadowy mists of time, with only a small percentage of primary material available for modern-day study. If only the camera had been invented earlier, who knows what intriguing images we would have of Wirral? We may have seen pictures of great battles fought out upon the epic fields of Bromborough, or shots of our oldest church in mid-construction on the banks of the River Mersey. We may have witnessed the devastating effects of the plague as it riddled our towns and villages, or seen the early ferries as they crossed the choppy waves to the markets of Liverpool. Such images are frustratingly confined to our nostalgic imaginations.

With the inevitable progression of time came the industrial Victorian era and, in turn, great advances in technology. It is from this enlightened period that we observe many of the depictions in this collection. These images, although only relatively young in terms of Wirral's overall history, showcase some of the intriguing architectural evolutions that have taken place within our beloved villages and towns over the past two centuries. They cast a remarkable light on our social history too, candidly capturing the people of the past, with their forms forever caught in that moment in history.

Today we are to enter a renaissance. The history of Wirral is soon to enter a new and exhilarating chapter; the development firm, Peel Holdings, is set to embark on the greatest building project the peninsula has ever seen. In this multibillion-pound project, Birkenhead docks are set to be transformed into a world-class waterfront, alive with an energy to rival the best cities in the world. This glorious scheme shall create upwards of 25,000 jobs and is likely to bring about the creation of many new streets and fantastic new buildings. The project is set to be completed in thirty years and I for one cannot wait to see the results.

As a genuine patriot of Wirral, I take great pleasure in being able to present to you *Wirral Then & Now*. It has been an honour to compile this work, and to play my part in preserving our area's history. My endless thanks go to Barney Finlayson for taking the time to produce these fantastic photographs of today, and to Ian and Marilyn Boumphrey – without their hard work and research this book would never have been possible.

I hope one day, far in the distant future, our descendents shall reflect back on our quaint, old-fashioned, twenty-first-century towns and muse fondly over their historic past: may they do so in a Wirral that, for now, we can only dream of.

Daniel K. Longman, 2011

CHARING CROSS AND GRANGE ROAD

THIS WAS THE view from the town centre's Charing Cross, in the early twentieth century. The curved Grange Hotel is located to the left of this picture and was owned by Thomas Lloyd. Looking closely, his name can be spotted inscribed above the pub's entrance, as two fashionable women pass by. Next door, at number 262, is Robert Roberts' tea dealership, with John Evan's butcher shop based alongside. Over the street, the tall and notable construction is a branch of the North and South Wales Bank, which was completed in 1902. The firm was set up in 1836 by several enterprising merchants, who felt Wales needed its own national bank. From their head office

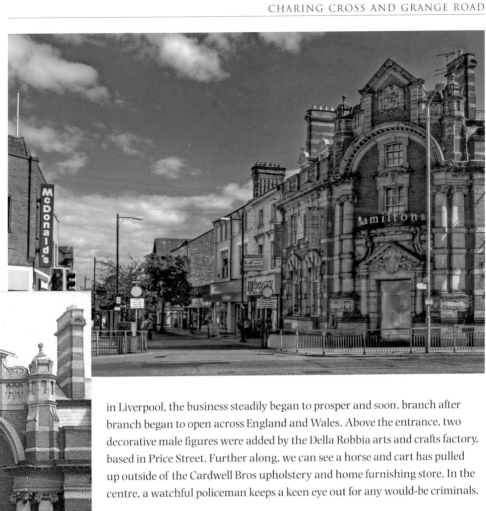

in Liverpool, the business steadily began to prosper and soon, branch after branch began to open across England and Wales. Above the entrance, two decorative male figures were added by the Della Robbia arts and crafts factory, based in Price Street. Further along, we can see a horse and cart has pulled up outside of the Cardwell Bros upholstery and home furnishing store. In the centre, a watchful policeman keeps a keen eye out for any would-be criminals.

TWENTY-FIRST-CENTURY Grange Road has altered a great deal since its Victorian heyday. The Grange Hotel was demolished in the 1980s and now the global fast food restaurant McDonald's occupies the site. The tea dealer's store has become Town Textiles, which sells a mixture of fabric and haberdashery, and the shop next door now offers discount clothing. The old North and South Wales Bank later became the Midland Bank and nowadays the firm is part of HSBC. The Grange Road building, however, is no longer associated to the banking profession and for several years has operated as a public house. Its most recent incarnation, Hamilton's, has closed and now the magnificent building awaits conversion into a stylish coffee house. Grange Road itself has also been transformed throughout the years. The main road that once ran through towards Argyle Street has been redesigned and totally pedestrianised, with paving slabs, benching and trees.

CHARING CROSS AND GRANGE ROAD WEST

THIS IS THE sister image to the previous Charing Cross shot; this time we are gazing out towards Grange Road West. The buildings to the right of this image were built in 1901 and were the work of architects Douglas and Minshull; the same designers of the many beautiful, mock-Tudor style buildings in Chester city centre. This gothic area in Birkenhead once housed a branch of the Bank of Liverpool, the entrance to which was through the arched doorway seen to the right, between the two towers. This whole section of buildings became known as 'Bank Buildings', as the Bank of Liverpool was in fact responsible for ordering its construction. It was built with a mixture of brick and ashlar stone, topped with a Westmoreland green slate roof. The shop alongside the bank was a branch of Holland & Sons, watchmakers that had a number of other stores situated in Bedford Road, Rock Ferry and across the river in Liverpool's Old Hall Street. Further along, into Grange Road

West, is the medicinal business Thompson & Capper, a firm specialising in homoeopathic remedies. Nearby, at numbers 2-4 Grange Road West, stands Thomas Murphy's wholesaler, selling wine and spirits.

SET AGAINST THE clear blue morning sky, the fairytale-like Bank Buildings appear as handsome as they did back in 1901. Today, hairstylist Christopher Boyton occupies the former Bank of Liverpool premises, as well as owning a second shop in Heswall. With his wife Kelly and their team of hairdressers, the Boytons have been styling the heads of Wirral for nearly thirty years. The watch-making shop of Mr Holland is now a type of pawnbrokers, specialising in gold and jewellery, and the old chemist store alongside is now operating as a small nail salon. Further down, the Charing Cross Hotel (one of the few surviving pubs in the area), can be seen operating from the former wholesale premises. Bank Buildings was made a Grade II listed site in 1974 and is one of the most interesting and unusual architectural spots that Wirral has on show.

ARGYLE STREET

THIS EARLY TWENTIETH-CENTURY view features a number of flat-capped individuals standing outside a public house, the George and Dragon, in Birkenhead town centre. The landlord at the time of this shot may well have been John Breeze, who is listed as the owner by 1914. The tall, dramatic construction that is the Argyle Theatre can be seen in the distance. The theatre was first opened on 21 December 1868 and its sought-after stage showcased various notable acts of the time, including Sir Harry Lauder, George Formby, Stan Laurel and the world-famous Charlie Chaplin. The Argyle became the Prince of Wales Theatre in 1876, but it was not long before she was re-christened her original moniker, reverting back to the Argyle fourteen years later. The manager, Dennis Clarke, was very proud of the fact that his theatre's vitagraph shows were the first such displays of moving

pictures outside of London, and also for owning the first theatre to broadcast on radio; it was the only theatre broadcasting to the USA at the time. Mr Clarke's establishment launched the careers of many emerging twentieth-century acts and helped put Birkenhead on the map, as the Argyle became one of the most well-known performance halls in the country.

THE POPULAR GEORGE and Dragon still stands as a licensed premises on this corner site, but the neighbouring theatre has long since vanished. The auditorium received a direct hit from the Nazi Luftwaffe on 21 September 1940, turning the once impressive venue into nothing but a burnt-out shell. It remained in that state for the next thirty years, before it was finally torn down in the 1970s. Today, nothing remains of the Argyle; a car park for House of Fraser, the department store, now covers the area. Argyle Street remains a busy area of the town, with drivers and pedestrians often taking the road to access the neighbouring conurbations of Tranmere, Bebington and Wallasey.

WILLIAMSON ART GALLERY

A LOOK AT the eastern side of the wonderful Williamson Art Gallery, located in sleepy Oxton's Slatey Road. The purpose-built museum and gallery was opened in 1928 to house local examples of professional artwork, such as famous Della Robbia pottery, Liverpudlian porcelain and numerous displays of Victorian paintings with links to the North West and North Wales. The construction is named after John and Patrick Williamson, a father and son duo who each donated a substantial sum of money to the Borough Council in the early part of the last century.

John was a local businessman who made a fortune as a director of the mighty Cunard Steamship Co. Ltd. It was partly his money which enabled Liverpool architects Messrs Hannaford & Thearle to design and build this neo-Georgian, single-storey building, which would become a much loved cultural attraction for the people of Wirral.

THE MUSEUM REMAINS open to the public, with an exterior largely unchanged in its almost one-hundred-year existence. Outside, the two trees have grown strong since their planting eighty years previously and the museum's gardens have greatly matured. The Williamson itself maintains a vigorous programme of contemporary art; this runs alongside displays from the museum's own exceptional pictorial collections, maritime displays, local history exhibitions and a fascinating motor museum, also within the building. The museum's temporary exhibitions are constantly being renewed and updated, making the gallery a popular visit for tourists from Wirral, Liverpool and other parts of the North West.

SEACOMBE FERRY TERMINAL

A BUSY SEACOMBE ferry terminal from 1933 (below), showcasing its brand new look. Before this time, a less impressive and much simpler terminal occupied the site. The first Wirral ferry service across the river began in medieval times, when Benedictine monks from Birkenhead made regular crossings. Over time, however, Seacombe and nearby Woodside grew to become the main points for a traveller's nautical endeavours. Throughout the early part of the twentieth century, many architectural improvements were made to this part of Wallasey and, at a cost of £107,000, these new terminal buildings underwent a complete transformation. The new construction featured booking rooms, waiting rooms, offices and workshops, all adorned in decorative brick and Portland stone. In this shot, various people can be seen around the terminal building preparing to make a trip across the Mersey, while others walk home after completing their cross-river journey. The large

terminal clock tower stands tall at a height of 90ft, looking down on the people of Wallasey and the increasingly popular and affordable motor cars below. By the time this image was taken, Seacombe Ferry was carrying thirty million passengers every year.

TODAY, THE IMPOSING tower of the terminal building makes an impressive sight and can been seen for miles around. During the First World War, two Mersey ferries, the *Iris* and the *Daffodil*, were instrumental during the Zeebrugge raid on the Belgium coast in 1918. The mission was to disrupt the movement of the feared U-Boats and interrupt the activities of German light shipping, which was becoming a serious problem for the Royal Navy. The two humble vessels acted as landing craft for marines and for HMS *Vindictive*, but both came under heavy fire. As a result of their valiant actions, King George V resolved that these ferries, and all such future ferries, should be honoured with the word 'Royal' in their title. Seacombe was also the first commercial shore-based radar station in the world, installed here in 1947. Cross-river ferries continue to operate from this location and the terminal has become an attraction in its own right. It now houses a small café, an aquarium and a futuristic attraction known as the Spaceport, which features a variety of out-of-this-world exhibits on the theme of space travel. It was opened in 2005 at a cost of £10m.

WALLASEY TOWN HALL

THE FOUNDATION STONE for this towering, renaissance-style hall was laid by King George V,
by the novel means of electricity, on 25 March 1914. A special platform was set up in Central
Park, with a connecting cable to the site in Brighton Street, nearly a mile away. The King simply
pressed a button and the foundation stone fell into place with hearty cheers from jubilant
onlookers. A Town Hall had originally been situated in Church Street since the mid-1800s,
but a new construction, with a glorious river-view location, was agreed upon at the turn of
the new century. The year 1913 had seen Wallasey become a borough in its own right, and it
was to be here, on the banks of the Mersey, that local councillors would eventually carry out

their important civic duties. It was another six years, however, before the building could be used for its intended purpose, as international conflict threw the building into the hands of the armed forces. The hall was taken over as a military hospital and was used to treat several thousand injured soldiers during the First World War. It is seen here from the rear; it was built 'back-to-front' to give a more impressive appearance to the Wallasey waterfront. It stands at a height of 180ft.

THE MAGNIFICENT CONSTRUCTION still stands proudly on the river's edge and has become the central focus for the whole of Wirral's municipal activity. In 2001, during repair work, a small capsule dating back to 1916 was discovered inside a copper urn; the urn had been removed from the roof of the Town Hall. Inside it, intrigued workers discovered a coin dating from 1905 and two old newspapers. When the repairs were completed, the capsule was returned to the urn along with some twenty-first-century artefacts for future generations to find. The hall itself is often hired out for civic occasions, such as weddings and conferences, and remains a key architectural focal point of the Wallasey area. It is an instantly recognisable feature on the peninsula's landscape, with the best views to be had from the Liverpool waterfront.

OXTON ROAD CONGREGATIONAL CHURCH

THE REMARKABLE FOUR-PINNACLE creation that is the Oxton Road Congregational Church is pictured here in the year 1922, at the junction of Woodchurch Road and Balls Road. It was built

between 1857 and 1858 by the talented architect William Cole; he also designed Birkenhead's St Anne Church in Beckwith Street. Over £5,000 was spent on the creation of the congregational church, with a further £2,500 spent on improvements during the 1880s. It is viewed here (left) from Oxton Road, with a series of well-lit shops positioned on either side of the street and a number of varied townspeople heading about their business.

THE CHURCH WAS tragically gutted by fire in February 1922, just one month after undergoing a splendid redecoration. It was carefully restored and reopened again in 1923, but over the years the once awe-inspiring building began to be forgotten, and it gradually fell into a terrible state of disrepair. For decades, the Grade II listed building was a truly dreadful eyesore, with broken windows, missing slates and no real purpose. A number of companies had sought to find a profitable use for the site, but none were financially viable. It was only recently that the church met with fortune once again and was resurrected to its former glory. The building is now the Wirral Christian Centre; it has been returned to its original function, as a place for religious worship.

LEASOWE LIGHTHOUSE

THE AGED LEASOWE lighthouse on Leasowe Common was built in 1763. It is noted for being Britain's oldest handmade, brick-built lighthouse still in existence and was in use right up until 1908, under the watchful eye of the only known female lighthouse keeper of the time, Mrs Williams. She and her husband had operated the Great Orme lighthouse in Llandudno prior to moving to Wirral, until Mr William's ill health forced his wife to work the tower with only the help of their young daughter. Historians believe that the foundations of the lighthouse are built upon bales of cotton retrieved from a shipwreck in the Georgian era. As the old image shows, the area

went on to become a popular spot for camping; a number of happy holidaymakers are enjoying the fresh Wirral air from their tents.

THIS 30-METRE-HIGH lighthouse ceased to function in 1908, at which time Mrs Williams moved into a nearby cottage and used the lighthouse as a unique location for her tea rooms. They proved to be an instant hit with visitors but, upon her death, the building fell into serious neglect. By the late twentieth century the lighthouse was in need of some considerable aesthetic attention so, in 1989, £30,000 was spent by the Borough Council to clean it up and make it fit for public use. Today, Leasowe lighthouse hosts guided tours and numerous special public events are listed on its calendar. There is also a visitor centre located within, packed full of information about Leasowe and the surrounding areas. The lighthouse also serves as a home to Wirral's coastal rangers and remains a focal point of the very scenic North Wirral Coastal Park.

LISCARD ROAD

LISCARD ROAD IN the early twentieth century (below). A number of local children, one with
a wheelbarrow, are taking a keen interest in the unusual presence of a photographer. To the
right is Liscard post office, shaded with an awning; a young child can be seen peering through
the floor-to-ceiling glass window. There is a mixture of stores occupying the length of this busy
Wallasey thoroughfare, which leads to Liscard; these include the North and South Wales Bank,
which can be seen in the distance at the corner of Westminster Road. Liscard's history dates back
many centuries, with the first known mention of the town as Lisnekarke, back in 1260. Due to the
creation of the ferry service, Liscard grew from a small village of just 211 people in 1801, to nearly

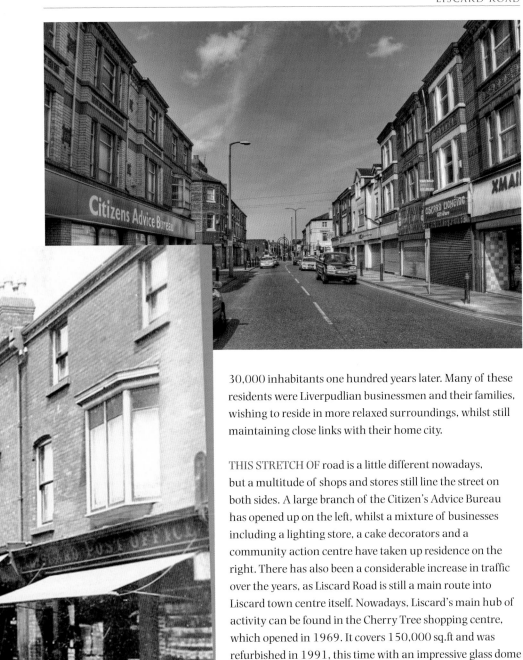

30,000 inhabitants one hundred years later. Many of these residents were Liverpudlian businessmen and their families, wishing to reside in more relaxed surroundings, whilst still maintaining close links with their home city.

THIS STRETCH OF road is a little different nowadays, but a multitude of shops and stores still line the street on both sides. A large branch of the Citizen's Advice Bureau has opened up on the left, whilst a mixture of businesses including a lighting store, a cake decorators and a community action centre have taken up residence on the right. There has also been a considerable increase in traffic over the years, as Liscard Road is still a main route into Liscard town centre itself. Nowadays, Liscard's main hub of activity can be found in the Cherry Tree shopping centre, which opened in 1969. It covers 150,000 sq.ft and was refurbished in 1991, this time with an impressive glass dome covering the whole development. According to the 2001 census, the town's population has decreased dramatically since the previous century, with only 14,000 recorded inhabitants.

RAKE LANE CEMETERY

THIS SOMBRE VIEW (below) depicts two boys and a gentleman in a bowler hat posing outside the sturdy stone entrance to Wallasey's Rake Lane Cemetery in 1916. In the late Victorian era, after much deliberation, a committee of officials purchased ten acres of suitable land and put it to use as much-needed burial space. Rake Lane Cemetery was officially opened for internments in 1883; within the grounds there are many historic tombs. It is the resting place of many unfortunate victims of national and local tragedies, including those who perished during the sinking of the *Titanic*, the *Empress of Ireland* and the hospital ship, *Lusitania*. Also buried under the soil are some of the unfortunate victims to the infamous Liverpool Bay *Thetis* disaster. Built at Cammell Lairds in 1938, the *Thetis* submarine conducted her final diving trials the following summer. It was during these tests that a series of tragic misunderstandings caused the vessel to sink when its torpedo hatches filled with water, the crew remaining oblivious. Lengthy rescue efforts could only save four of the 103 men who were left inside the vessel, the majority of whom died through a lack of oxygen. Cornelius Smith and John Griffiths were two engine fitters from the shipyard who would later be interred in this cemetery.

THE CEMETERY REMAINS in existence but outgrew its boundaries some time ago, forcing the local authorities to set up further burial grounds elsewhere around the neighbourhood. There are now nine sites run by Wirral Borough Council. The original walls and stone pillars of Rake

Lane remain in place, as does the unassuming chapel, which can be seen in the distance. The chapel has evolved and become a Russian Orthodox Church; it hosted its first wedding in April

2010. An investment of £30,000 was recently put towards its refurbishment and towards the completion of other improvements to the chapel grounds. These included the installation of new perimeter fencing and other security measures to keep the cemetery free from vandalism and ill-use. In 2005, Wirral-born war hero Flight Sergeant Ray Holmes was laid to rest at Rake Lane. In 1940 he successfully prevented an attack on Buckingham Palace when he rammed his Hurricane fighter into a German Dornier bomber during a tense dogfight over the London skies. Both planes crashed to the ground, but Holmes was able to bail out at the last second and won the respect of the British public for his heroic and selfless actions.

CHURCH ROAD

SEVERAL INQUISITIVE YOUNGSTERS can be seen in this depiction of Tranmere's Church Road
from 1912. A rather quaint church compared to some others in Wirral, St Catherine's is seen
behind the group alongside a tramcar, as it makes its journey from Birkenhead. The church was
founded in 1831 thanks to W. Hough Esq., who donated the land to the local people. Until then, the
residents of Tranmere were forced to walk to the church of St Andrew in Bebington and worship
there. St Catherine's began life as a small and simple brick building with rather basic rectangular
windows and only a small tower. In the 1870s the building was substantially improved, with
additions including the then sky-scraping spire than can be seen in the photograph. To the left
is the much-feared Birkenhead Union Workhouse, which first received inmates in 1864. It was
designed to keep the able-bodied inspired to work; conditions inside for those that refused were

most unpleasant. Its grounds covered a large stretch of Church Road and also the parallel thoroughfare of Yolk of Egg Lane, later christened Derby Road. The black-and-white brick building to the right is the St Catherine's Church Institute, erected in 1892, comprising of two halls that seat over 600 patrons between them.

ST CATHERINE'S CHURCH survives as one of the last focal points in this part of Tranmere, as many of its contemporary buildings have fallen foul to demolition. Government regeneration projects have seen this part of Wirral flattened, with many of the derelict buildings of old removed from view. The workhouse has become St Catherine's Community Hospital and is one of a number of places that provides healthcare to the people of Wirral. Plans for a brand new hospital are currently underway in a £28m scheme that will provide a new home for the medical services in the aged Victorian buildings. The old tramlines have been torn up, with no trace of the once integral part of Tranmere's transportation system remaining. The Tudor-style Institute still stands in its original location alongside a plot of land currently used for allotments. It remains in use as a public hall.

DUKE STREET AND PARK ROAD NORTH

HERE WE SEE the junction of Duke Street and Park Road North in an early twentieth-century shot of Birkenhead. The corner building is a grocery store owned by the enterprising Williams Brothers. They owned several such stores across the borough; their well-known name is in clear view above the shop doorway. Next door is a post office and sweet shop and further along stands the property of Arthur Hignett, whose drapers advertisement can be seen printed high upon the bricks of the building. Outside is a lone cart; it seems to be the only traffic in the street. Further down the road is the Duke Street Bridge, which joins the two halves of Wirral together over the docks that are known as the East and West Floats. The bridge was opened in the 1860s as one of the world's largest bascule bridges, allowing vessels in and out of the busy River Mersey as and when necessary.

AS THIS MODERN-DAY image shows, the area around Duke Street and Park Road North is still recognisable, despite going through a number of noticeable changes. The Williams Brothers grocery store has changed hands many times through the years and is now a branch of the William Hill bookmakers. The former residential part of this old house, which was downstairs, has completely vanished, with the front door and hedge no longer remaining. The bookmakers have also taken over the former post office property, giving the betting shop a larger interior. Looking up, the advert of Arthur Hignett has been removed and now a pizza and kebab house occupies the site. At the roadside, no less than three sets of traffic lights are situated on this corner alone. Duke Street and the bridge now function as a main route to Wallasey and the seaside town of New Brighton.

THORNTON HOUGH

THE VILLAGE OF Thornton Hough dates back many hundreds of years; it was listed as 'Toritone' in William the Conquerors' Domesday Book of 1086. Its current name, however, was only established when the daughter of local landowner, Roger de Thornton, married Richard de Hoghe during the reign of Edward II. This Victorian shot below shows a group of children playing with what appears to be an upturned bench on the village green. Thornton Hough was developed by Joseph Hirst in the 1860s. He also constructed All Saints' Church, a vicarage, a school and housing, including the exquisite row known as Wilshaw Terrace. Lord Lever added his own architectural mark to the village in the late 1880s. He updated some of Hirst's inadequate cottages, transforming them into the stylish half-timbered homes as seen in this photograph from 1892. A second school was built to help meet the growing demand, as was another church called St George's.

THE HOUSES THAT line the village green are known as the Folds and were designed by Lever's architects from Port Sunlight; they were built to resemble traditional almshouses. The village green, seen here (right) being used for a game of football, is a 3.3-hectare area; it is the main focal

point of village life. It provides a picturesque venue for all manner of sports and leisure activities. Every year since 2004, it has won the Green Flag Award, which recognises and rewards the best green spaces the UK has to offer. It is the only village green in the country to boast this impressive accolade. Just out of shot stands a playground, very popular with children on sunny days, as well as tennis courts and a Grade II listed pavilion. Each year the village hosts an annual scarecrow festival, where members of the public create their own weird and wonderful scarecrows and place them around the village. The event is very popular and has become famous in its own right. Due to the villages' beauty, the local authority employs around eight members of staff to keep Thornton Hough in a tidy, attractive condition and to help keep its coveted status as one of the genuine jewels of the peninsula.

THE DIAMOND

THIS VIEW SHOWS the splendid and beautiful boulevard of Port Sunlight, known as the Diamond, with several local employees enjoying their tranquil surroundings. A floral and architectural gem, this landscape was built in the centre of the model village in the early years of the twentieth

century and has always been one of Wirral's most popular attractions. In the foreground is an ornamental arch, erected in 1933, which frames the village's magnificent war memorial. The architect was Welshman William Goscombe John, personal friend to the village founder, Lord William Hesketh Lever (later titled Lord Leverhulme). Lever wished for a memorial to be built in honour of the Lever Brothers' soap work employees who gave their lives during the First World War. The impressive monument was finally completed in 1921 and is regarded as one of the greatest outside of London. At the far end of the Diamond stands the Lady Lever Art Gallery, built in 1922 and opened by Queen Victoria's youngest daughter, Princess Beatrice. It housed the best of Lord Lever's personal art collection.

THE VILLAGE OF Port Sunlight draws in thousands of visitors from all over the world every year and is seen as one of the greatest Victorian villages in existence. The Diamond remains in fantastic floral splendour and is now part of a much-loved conservation area. Its surrounding buildings, totalling nearly 900, are all Grade II listed, with some sections of the village included on the English Heritage Register of Parks and Gardens of Special Historic Interest list. The Lady Lever Art Gallery now houses an even greater multitude of works, including what is accepted to be the best collection of Wedgwood jasperware in the world and some of the finest Chinese art in the country. The gallery also boasts the best group of New Sculpture works outside of London and a collection of world famous pre-Raphaelite paintings. This view from the ornamental arch has hardly changed in the eighty years since it was built, and is still as beautiful.

WOODCHURCH ROAD SCHOOL

WOODCHURCH ROAD SCHOOL pictured below in the year 1904. This was the year the school opened in its new and larger location, having moved from Bennett's Hill, further down the street. The old school was only a simple and temporary building, constructed from iron in 1901. From there, the pupils carried out their studies for only three years before being relocated to the bigger, and clearly more adequate, premises as seen in the photograph. This new school could accommodate approximately 600 children with relative ease. Two finely dressed women can be seen waiting outside the school at the railings with their prams, as a multitude of children play in the yard. This chocolate-box scene was totally destroyed one night in May 1941; the school suffered dreadful damage during a Second World War air raid. Eight people died when a public shelter, based in the school playground, collapsed and crushed the unfortunate people within.

THIS PART OF Woodchurch Road is now solely used as a primary school and the building itself has remained largely unchanged. The main difference to be found is the unfortunate loss of the pinnacle from the school's once elevated tower. Today the school uses the ground floor to teach the younger members on its register while a mezzanine above is used for the school library and cooking facilities. The second floor is currently used for teaching the elder, Key Stage 2 pupils the National Curriculum with core subjects being English, maths, science and ICT. Woodchurch Road Primary School also offers its 450 pupils a number of extracurricular activities including Spanish, Latin, football, cricket, gymnastics and cooking, to name but a few. In recent years steps to improve the quality of the playground have been taken, with some of the colourful results seen in this image.

CLIFTON CRESCENT

THIS IS A mid-twentieth century view of Birkenhead's Clifton Crescent as it sits at the junction of Borough Road and Argyle Street. To the left of this shot is the Central Hotel, which was built in 1938 by the firm Lloyd & Cross. The exquisite clock tower seen standing in the centre was commissioned in 1911 as a memorial to Edward VII. He had died the previous year after suffering from severe bronchitis. Liverpool architect Edmund Kirby was asked to design the timepiece in fine Portland Stone, and its construction was completed a year later. Edward VII had opened Hamilton Square railway station on an official royal visit in January 1886, under his title of that time, the Prince of Wales; he was held in high regard by the people of Wirral ever since. The impressive clock tower had first been located on a nearby site over by Birkenhead Central

station but, in 1929, officials were forced to move it to make way for the exciting new project that was the Mersey tunnel approach road. People can be seen enjoying a moment's peace as they sit beneath the clock tower, with its adorning lion sculptures looking on.

THE MODEST CENTRAL Hotel has survived the economic pitfalls of recent years and continues to provide convenient accommodation to the multitude of visitors that flock to Merseyside. Inside, it contains twenty-nine en suite bedrooms, a restaurant and a well-stocked bar. The Edward VII memorial clock tower remains one of Birkenhead's most important architectural features and continues to stand in its Clifton Crescent location. The once pleasant sitting area around it, however, is no longer accessible for public use and has undergone a transformation into a busy roundabout. It is often laden with traffic emerging from the Queensway tunnel, which was completed in 1934. Edward VII's son, King George V, and his consort Queen Mary, took part in the opening ceremony and officially declared the revolutionary tunnel open to the public. It is just over two miles long and connects Birkenhead to Liverpool via an underwater passage beneath the River Mersey. It still remains the chief mode of transport between the two conurbations.

MANOR ROAD

WALLASEY'S MANOR ROAD and its central police station, at the corner of Queen Street. This distinguished building was opened in the year 1900 at a cost of £11,000, which was met by Cheshire County Council. Inside, several judicial courtrooms were conveniently constructed for local magistrates to try the criminal delinquents of Wallasey and the surrounding areas, after being captured by their police colleagues. These in-house courts, however, were not completed for another six years, at which point Wallasey's magisterial proceedings moved to the Manor Road building from the court of Liscard Road. The move forced the earlier establishment, which had by then served as a criminal court for nearly a century, to become redundant. It was later transformed into a weights and measures business and, after that, into a 400-seat cinema. The new Manor Road police station housed several small cells where anxious prisoners were kept as they awaited their fate. It also featured a new parade room that was used by the building's growing number

of policing personnel. In 1913, Wallasey's very own police force was formed to help tackle the mounting levels of crime emerging on Britain's streets.

IN 1972 THE ornate police premises were officially acquired from the Cheshire Police Authority and became the property of the Wirral Council; this was following a municipal restructure brought about by the Local Government Act. In 2010, the building was one of a number of properties featured in the Council's money-saving plans to raise funds through the sale of its assets, in an attempt to save over £1m a year. Inside, parts of the old courtrooms and cells still exist, but much of the late Victorian construction has been converted into offices; most recently a community safety team has occupied them. The dedicated men and women of the Wallasey police force became a part of the brand new Merseyside Police when most of the Liverpool and Bootle, Cheshire and Lancashire constabularies merged together in 1974. In February 2010, Merseyside Police's new Chief Constable, Jon Murphy, paid a visit to the current base of the Wallasey Police, a large twentieth-century building several yards up from the original, on his very first day on the job. He wanted to inspect Wirral constables and observe the working conditions of his diligent members of staff here on the peninsula.

HAMILTON SQUARE

THE MAGNIFICENT HAMILTON Square has been described as the jewel in Wirral's crown since its celebrated foundation. Built in 1826 by leading Edinburgh architect James Gillespie Graham, it was the brainchild and dream of entrepreneur William Laird. It was his vision to build a new and respectable town near to his flourishing shipyard on the banks of the Mersey. Hamilton Square was to be the centre, lined with elegant houses and luscious private gardens for the enjoyment of the new well-to-do of Wirral society. Space was left on a prime spot for the addition of a noble Town hall, on which work was begun in 1883. Birkenhead Town Hall was finally opened four years later by Laird's young daughter, Elsie; around 5,000 spectators gathered to watch. This early twentieth-century view shows the hall in all its glory, complete with its iconic 200ft clock tower. It was built with Scottish granite, local Storeton sandstone and topped with Welsh slate, adhering to the design of Charles Ellison. In front stands the remarkable and regal monument to Queen Victoria, which was commissioned to Edmund Kirby and unveiled in 1905. The £1,400 costs were generously, but mournfully, financed by public subscription; it was completed in the fitting style of a stunning Eleanor Cross.

HAMILTON SQUARE REMAINS one of the most beautiful parts of Birkenhead and still appears as elegant as ever. It continues to be one of the country's grandest public squares; only London's Trafalgar Square can boast more Grade I listed buildings in any one area. The private gardens were acquired by the local authority in 1903 and since then have been open to the public. In addition to the Queen Victoria Monument, there is also the town's cenotaph, which was unveiled to a colossal crowd on 5 July 1925. The decision to remove the statue of the town founder, John Laird, which was originally situated in front of the Town Hall, was not taken lightly, but it was decided that the cenotaph should take pride of place. Each November many people gather to pay their respects to fallen servicemen who gave their lives for their country. The square is no longer home to the area's wealthy elite; most of the grand houses of the past have been converted into flats and apartments. The Town Hall, once an important political powerhouse, became a museum and registry office, with the borough administration moved to Wallasey. Now, the future of the building remains uncertain and the Council's financial state hinders any possible plans and progress. It is hoped that the hall shall once again be put to public use as a multi-arts community centre, studio and theatre in the near future.

THE WHEATSHEAF INN

THIS PHOTOGRAPH OF the Wheatsheaf Inn, located in the small hamlet of Raby, was taken in approximately 1900 and shows the centuries-old building on Raby Mere Road. It was long thought that the Wheatsheaf had been a public house since 1611 and a date mark, found inscribed on a gable during alterations, confirms this. However, further research has discovered that a farm, licensed to brew and sell beer since the thirteenth century, once covered this area. This makes the site one of the oldest hostelries in the country. The inn has been locally known as the Thatch for many years, due to its notable thatched roof, once a common sight on many properties in the neighbourhood. Raby Mere Road was the main passage between Birkenhead and Neston, so it was only natural that an inn be there to supply weary travellers with a place to rest and get refreshment. This image shows the charming inn itself, with its small adjoining cowshed. At the

rear of the property is an authentic Georgian barn dating from 1730, further adding to the exceptional historic value of this hidden part of Wirral.

THE WHEATSHEAF INN has been described by local media as the best kept secret in Wirral and has become a highly respected and well-visited countryside restaurant. It is in fact probably the oldest pub in Wirral. Today, the establishment carries on its 700-year-old tradition of ale supply and continues to stock a full menu of drinks to quench the needs of thirsty customers. Recent alterations have seamlessly merged the adjacent, and once redundant, cowshed into an adjoining restaurant. The aptly named Cowshed has become as popular as the inn itself; its olde-worlde charm compliments the traditional pub menu, which offers plenty of meat dishes and hearty vegetables. Diners can enjoy their meals beneath the inn's genuine wooden beams, or enjoy the weather outside in the restaurant's floral garden and terrace. Despite several refurbishments over the years, the historic thatched roof has survived in fine form, and the exterior of the building remains authentic and in excellent condition.

WOODSIDE FERRY TERMINAL

THIS PANORAMIC VIEW of Birkenhead's Woodside ferry terminal was photographed at the turn of the twentieth century from the Woodside Hotel. In 1330 King Edward III officially granted ferry rights to the monks of the nearby Birkenhead Priory, but they had provided passage and accommodation to travellers going to Lancashire for a number of years previously. The wooden ferry terminal shown in the photograph dates from the mid-1800s and can be seen with the large brick buildings of Woodside railway station standing alongside. It was said that the station exhibited some of the finest examples of Victorian railway architecture of its day. On the approach a number of horse-drawn cabs are waiting to pick up passengers disembarking from the ferry along with a lone tramcar. In 1860, Europe's first ever tramway was established here and ran from Woodside to Birkenhead Park. The idea was a great success and went on to become a national form of transport. The waters of the River Mersey are seen here busy with shipping traffic as ships and luggage boats make their way across the water and out into the Irish Sea.

THE GREATEST NUMBER of passengers at Woodside was on 20 May 1918, when 92,789 passengers travelled on the ferries. Nowadays the ferries are more of a tourist attraction than a mode of transport; the 1960s hit 'Ferry Cross the Mersey' by Gerry & the Pacemakers helped to seal this status. Woodside railway station was very busy right up until the 1960s, boasting a regular direct route to London Paddington. Later reassessment by the British Railway Board found the station to be surplus to requirements, as Liverpool's Lime Street station could provide the same services. By 1970 the station had been demolished, with little trace of it now remaining. In 2010 a £5m exhibition covering the history of a recovered Second World War German U-Boat was installed at the ferry terminal. She was recovered near the Danish island of Anholt after being sunk by an RAF bomber. Number U-534 is only one of four remaining such vessels in the world and has been dissected within the grounds of a specially built viewing platform. This allows enthralled visitors a unique insight into this once feared machine. This area of Birkenhead has been recognised as a prime site for development; there are plans in motion to capitalise on the exceptional views that Woodside has to offer.

WHETSTONE LANE

TRANMERE'S WHETSTONE LANE in the year 1907; several locals pose casually for the photographer. Lining the street to the right is a number of terraced houses, which would no doubt have had commanding views over Holt Hill and Argyle Street South. The steep gradient of Argyle Street South caused immense problems to tram engineers at this time. They were forced to construct a new approach through Pearson Road in order to access Whetstone Lane and the associated routes. Earlier, in the 1700s, Whetstone Lane was one of the important routes taken by a six-horsed coach carrying travellers to and from the town. It ran from Woodside to Chester and Parkgate three days a week, via the main passage of Old Chester Road. To the left is the

high stone wall of the Holt Hill Convent. This estate was a large private home of solicitor Henry Walker until 1856, when it was purchased by the Faithful Companions of Jesus and opened as an all-girls' boarding school. At the time this photograph was taken the holy nuns were teaching fifty female boarders and a hundred day pupils.

THE OLD TERRACED houses to the right on Whetstone Lane, including an old hairdresser's, have since been demolished and now only vacant grassland remains. One sole property occupies the site once used by a laundry in the early 1900s, with a brightly coloured newsagent's store positioned a short distance away. The black and white bollards continue to prevent access to the steep hill of Argyle Street South but modern day vehicles have no problem in reaching the summit. The Holt Hill Convent ceased to house boarders in the 1930s and in the following decade became a Grammar school. In 1976 the school amalgamated with Heathley High School, a comprehensive girls' school, and became known as Marian High School. This school was relocated in the 1980s and the old Victorian building was demolished. Many of the important pieces within were donated to other institutions, such as the chapel crucifix, which now hangs in St Joseph's Church, and the stained-glass windows, which can now be seen in St Paul's. Today, semi-detached houses stand in the former grounds in the suitably named Convent and Rectory Close.

THE BOATHOUSE,
BIRKENHEAD PARK

THIS LATE NINETEENTH-century view shows the stately Roman-style boathouse situated in Birkenhead's world famous public park, on the bank of the east lake. Its construction began in 1843 and was finally completed four years later. The surroundings are carved from former swampland; this involved approximately 1,000 men draining and laying out the land. Joseph Paxton designed the boathouse, as well as the park, which was to have a bandstand with a pavilion and three segmental-arched openings divided by grand pilasters. During the celebrations for the park's official opening in 1847, a performance by the Lancashire bell ringers tunefully added to the day's merry celebrations in the boathouse. There was to be a second bandstand situated in the lower park, not far from Canon Hill, an area named after the two Russian cannons that had been captured during the Crimean War. In 1885 a third circular cast-iron

bandstand was erected in the park and featured regular weekly evening performances by various bands in the summer seasons. The boathouse is seen here surrounded by mature trees and shrubbery above the calm waters of the serpentine lake.

THIS WONDERFUL SUMMER view (above) of Birkenhead Park's beautiful boathouse shows the Classical structure at its best. In 2002 the park received £11.5m from the Heritage Lottery Fund. With this, developers successfully refurbished the whole park, including the boathouse; the results can be seen in this image. Yorkshire-based building contractors William Anelay was asked to restore several aspects of the park, including the grand entrance lodge, the Swiss bridge and, of course, the boathouse, which needed several modifications. It was in very poor condition and required extensive masonry work to repair the damages it had sustained through its 150-year history. This included the installation of a brand new tiled roof, which has now been accomplished. The cool waters of the lakes have been cleaned and restocked with the addition of 23,000 skimmer bream, roach, tench, crucian carp and gudgeon. A small number of concrete platforms have been constructed at the edge of the lakes to allow easier access for Wirral's anglers, who enjoy the occasional spot of fishing in the park. The area's wide variety of existing shrubs and trees were pruned back and the sowing of new seeds and plants has helped make Birkenhead Park a fine public space, one that England can be proud of once again.

35 OXTON ROAD

THIS PHOTOGRAPH SHOWS the terrible damage done to Charles Dashley's butcher shop in Oxton Road. Charles (real name Karl Deuschle) was a German national who, by 1896, had moved to Britain seeking a better life. At number 35 he had set up shop as a pork butcher, but in May of 1915 the people of Birkenhead turned against him. That month saw some of the worst riots the town had ever seen, due to the fact that the Cunard ocean liner, *Lusitania*, was annihilated off the coast of Ireland. U-Boat U20, under the control of Kapitänleutnant Walther Schwieger, fired a torpedo at the hospital ship, causing her to sink in only eighteen minutes. The attack claimed the lives of nearly 1,200 passengers from both sides of the Atlantic and caused a widespread public

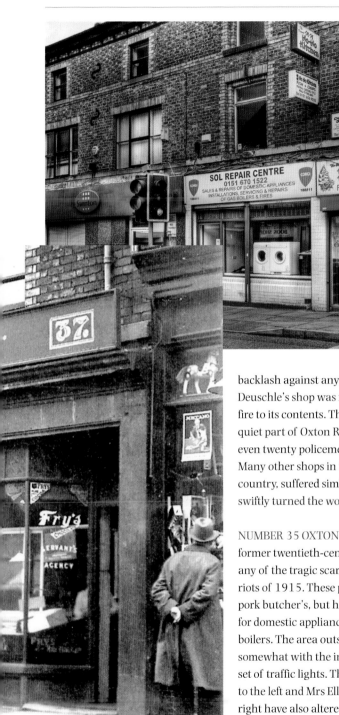

backlash against anyone suspected of German origin. Mr Deuschle's shop was ransacked as crowds broke in and set fire to its contents. That eventful day turned this normally quiet part of Oxton Road into a scene of utter bedlam; even twenty policemen found it hard to control the chaos. Many other shops in the area, and indeed across the whole country, suffered similar fates as Germany's naval actions swiftly turned the world against them.

NUMBER 35 OXTON Road bears little resemblance to its former twentieth-century appearance, nor does it exhibit any of the tragic scars it received during the chaotic riots of 1915. These premises also no longer operate as a pork butcher's, but have instead become a repair centre for domestic appliances such as washing machines and boilers. The area outside the shop has also changed somewhat with the installation of a public crossing and a set of traffic lights. The old shops of John Duff the baker to the left and Mrs Ellen James' confectionary store to the right have also altered. The insurance company Swinton occupies numbers 33-35, whilst a Chinese takeaway stands at number 37.

BEDFORD ROAD AND NEW CHESTER ROAD JUNCTION

ROCK FERRY IS shown here in the late nineteenth century at the junction of Bedford Road and New Chester Road. This area of Rock Ferry was heavily developed by the middle classes in the mid-1800s; the well-to-do Rock Park estate was constructed at this time. This was partly thanks to the introduction of nearby steam ferries, allowing quick and easy access to Liverpool from the Wirral shoreline. Rock Park became a highly sought after residence, designed and paid for by a team of stock merchants known as the Rock Ferry Company. The most famous resident of the estate was Nathaniel Hawthorne, the American author and US Consul to Liverpool, who lived at number 26. Here, Bedford Road was named after the Prime Minister Lord John Russell, whose historic family seat was at Bedford. The thoroughfare can be seen here with a branch of the London and City Midland Bank positioned to the left and William Pollard's boot and shoe

shop, complete with an eye-catching window display, to the right. A second bank, Parr's, can be spotted to the immediate right of the photographer and a policeman stands on guard in the centre of shot.

LOOKING AT THIS part of Rock Ferry today you'll see noticeable differences. The outer shell of the former shoe and boot shop no longer exists and instead there is the simple, box-like building that was once beneath; it is now the home of Wirral Lifelong Learning Services. They provide and develop educational courses for local people who need help in certain areas, including Maths and English, which are provided free of charge. Across the street the old London and City Midland Bank building is still standing at its corner location but under a new guise. It is now known as Outlook House; the name is positioned high above the door by the two original and beautifully carved classical figures. The cotton experts, Cotton Outlook, now run a weekly news journal from the premises, providing the latest information to cotton merchants in over one hundred countries around the globe. Looking up Bedford Road, several properties have been lost over the years, but the area has recently been targeted by the Government Newheartlands scheme, aimed at improving the social and environmental aspects of Wirral's less affluent areas.

WOODSIDE HOTEL

THIS IMAGE WAS captured in the summer of July 1913 and shows the Woodside Hotel behind a group of Wirral naval volunteers heading towards the ferry terminal. The men were on their way to take part in a parade through the streets of Liverpool, where they would march past the King and Queen, who had paid a special royal visit, at St George's Hall. The hotel was originally built in the 1830s as a large and prominent coaching house with enough room for approximately one hundred horses. It had been constructed on or near to the site of an earlier property, known as the Woodside Ferry Boathouse, from where coaches would run to Chester three days a week. At one time the waves of the Mersey washed up very near to the Woodside Hotel, which had a small wooden runway leading into the water for the docking of small boats. In later years this slipway was developed and by 1840 a much-improved stone jetty was constructed. It also became a popular walking spot for people coming to stroll along the shoreline in more pleasant weather. The soaring tower in the background belongs to Hamilton Square train station. This was built to contain

10,000 gallons of water in order to move the luxury hydraulic lifts to and from its underground platforms.

AFTER NEARLY 200 years of trading, the Woodside Hotel was gutted by fire in 2008, causing thousands of pounds of damage to the pub in, what police investigators believed to be, a criminal attack. The following August, a second blaze ripped through the derelict three-storey building, causing the structure to be deemed unsafe. Diligent fire crews remained on the scene tackling the inferno, but it was too late for the hotel to be saved. With concern for public safety paramount, demolition crews later moved into action and carefully demolished the precarious historic hazard and, with it, part of the town's heritage. Today the site remains empty, but there are hopeful strategies in motion to see the whole area heavily redeveloped. It is anticipated that the initial plans will feature an outline for a new 'development spine' running from the Woodside Ferry terminal up to Hamilton Square station, with fresh new bars, restaurants and leisure areas gracing the vicinity. Planners and officials hope to help drive the regeneration of Wirral in the coming years through the epic Wirral Waters scheme and by making the most out of Woodside's truly unique location and fantastic views.

BRIDGE INN

PORT SUNLIGHT'S BRIDGE Inn as it was in its opening year, 1900. This photograph was taken from the west side of the property, as seen from Church Drive. The architects Edward Ould and George Grayson designed the picturesque inn; the former was an expert in black and white style architecture. Many more examples of this work can be found all over the village. The inn is situated in Bolton Road; a main street named after William Lever's hometown. It started out as a completely sober establishment, following the philosophy of the temperance movement. It refused to stock alcohol of any kind. However, the hardworking employees of the Sunlight Soap works grew thirsty and, in 1903, begged Lever for a village referendum. This was begrudgingly granted and the residents voted 80 per cent in favour of a liquor licence for the inn. The building's old style charm was appreciated by villagers and visitors alike, who appreciated the inn's dining environment, tea and guest rooms. The Bridge Inn takes its title from the nearby Victoria Bridge, which had opened three years earlier in honour of the Queen and spanned the village's tidal creek.

TODAY THE BRIDGE Inn is a successful pub, as well as being one of the many bed and breakfasts providing excellent hospitality to the 300,000 visitors who come to Port Sunlight every year. Over the decades a number of improvements and refurbishments have been made, including the addition of a brand new wing, giving the establishment a total of eleven bedrooms. All are complete with mod cons, helping to make a guest's stay in Port Sunlight a pleasure. As with many aged UK pubs, the Bridge Inn has a reputation for being haunted; the ghostly figures of a soldier, a merchant seaman, a young servant girl and a distinguished gentleman smoking a cigar have all reportedly been seen by pub patrons throughout the years. Nevertheless, the Bridge Inn provides an excellent location from which visitors can explore the village and the rest of Wirral. It was deservedly granted a Grade II listed status in the 1960s and the marvellous architecture, inside and out, never fails to impress. The main building has hardly changed since its completion but, as the image above shows, the once abundant grassland around the perimeter has been laid with tarmac and transformed into parking spaces for the inn's numerous guests and visitors.

GRANGE ROAD

BIRKENHEAD'S MAIN SHOPPING street, Grange Road, in the year 1935. This formerly quiet and wooded stretch of road was once known as Grange Lane and was used by the town's monks to move food and other produce from a grange that was situated on the outskirts of Oxton. From there, stock was taken aboard their ferries and shipped across the river, where it was sold to the increasingly populous town of Liverpool. This image shows a branch of the enterprising Irwin's Grocers to the left of the road. From humble beginnings this small family business prospered and the name Irwin's became a common sight all over the North West and beyond. Woolworths occupied the tall brick property alongside. New York-born Frank Woolworth set up his first

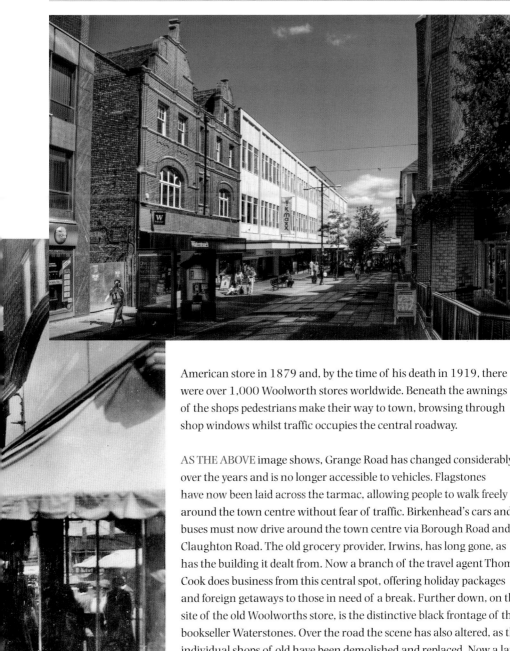

American store in 1879 and, by the time of his death in 1919, there were over 1,000 Woolworth stores worldwide. Beneath the awnings of the shops pedestrians make their way to town, browsing through shop windows whilst traffic occupies the central roadway.

AS THE ABOVE image shows, Grange Road has changed considerably over the years and is no longer accessible to vehicles. Flagstones have now been laid across the tarmac, allowing people to walk freely around the town centre without fear of traffic. Birkenhead's cars and buses must now drive around the town centre via Borough Road and Claughton Road. The old grocery provider, Irwins, has long gone, as has the building it dealt from. Now a branch of the travel agent Thomas Cook does business from this central spot, offering holiday packages and foreign getaways to those in need of a break. Further down, on the site of the old Woolworths store, is the distinctive black frontage of the bookseller Waterstones. Over the road the scene has also altered, as the individual shops of old have been demolished and replaced. Now a large shopping centre, known as the Pyramids, covers the area. The former big names of old, such as Tutty's, Robb Brothers and, of course, Irwins, no longer exist in Birkenhead, as the likes of Topshop, TK Maxx and Next dominate the high street.

WOODCHURCH ROAD

STEPPING BACK THROUGH the years to the turn of the last century, we take a look at rural Woodchurch Road in Prenton. This road led to the suburb of Woodchurch, a small centre of arable farmland with about one hundred listed residents. The property in shot is the brick-built Halfway House, which once catered for the various somnolent travellers making their way through this sleepy pastoral hamlet; it is named as such because of its convenient midway location between the neighbourhoods of Woodside and Woodchurch. Its advertisement for alcohol can just be seen high upon the side of the building. Just out of shot is a small sign for Storeton Road, a little village just over a mile away. Outside the inn a horse and cart trots off up the road in the direction of Arrowe Park. The Halfway House was just one of a small number of

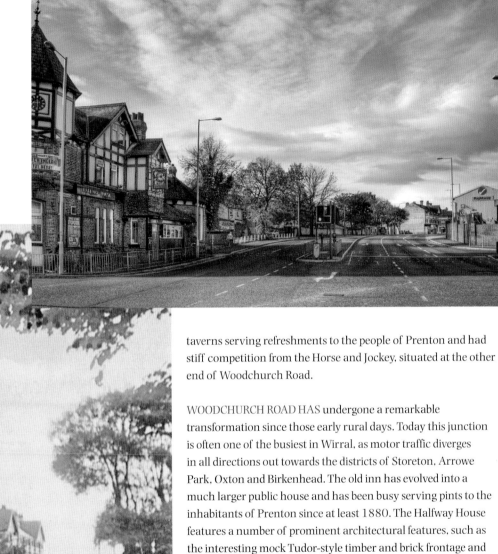

taverns serving refreshments to the people of Prenton and had stiff competition from the Horse and Jockey, situated at the other end of Woodchurch Road.

WOODCHURCH ROAD HAS undergone a remarkable transformation since those early rural days. Today this junction is often one of the busiest in Wirral, as motor traffic diverges in all directions out towards the districts of Storeton, Arrowe Park, Oxton and Birkenhead. The old inn has evolved into a much larger public house and has been busy serving pints to the inhabitants of Prenton since at least 1880. The Halfway House features a number of prominent architectural features, such as the interesting mock Tudor-style timber and brick frontage and the clock tower, making the building one of the most recognisable pubs in the area. It is open to the general public seven days a week, serving food and drink all day long. Much like the earlier image, advertisements for beer are also on show on the outside of the building but, with the advances in technology, landlords and publicans can now tempt their customers with product photography. Storeton Road is still to the left side of the brickwork, which has also been totally redeveloped with numerous late Victorian and Edwardian properties now lining the street.

NEW BRIGHTON BEACH

NEW BRIGHTON AND its beach have been popular places to visit for generations. The town was the creation of Liverpool merchant James Atherton, who brought nearly 200 acres of land to develop a rival to the much-respected royal playground of Brighton in the early eighteenth century. He envisioned grand houses, large gardens and reputable residents, but sure enough New Brighton became a resort for the working classes, who came in their masses to enjoy the fresh sea air and open spaces. This image (below) from 1902 captures one such day at the beach; a mass of formerly dressed people are strolling along the sand. In the distance stands the New Brighton Fort, which was built in 1829 at a cost of just under £27,000. Fear of a Napoleonic attack upon the city of Liverpool forced officials to make plans to protect the strategic seaport. Sixteen large mounted guns were installed about the defensive battery, along with enough accommodation to house one hundred military personnel. By the time this image was taken, the importance of the fort as a military outpost had declined, but it still processed the deadly artillery to fire upon enemy vessels entering our waters.

VISITING NEW BRIGHTON now, you cannot fail to notice that the golden sands of the past now lie several feet under water. In the 1930s, Wirral Council built an artificial marine lake as part of the King's Parade, on reclaimed land. It now covers a large part of the old seashore. The sturdy fort, known as Perch Rock, remains intact but no longer has any military use. In 1939, fifteen

minutes after the announcement of war, Fort Commander Cocks gave the order for two shots
to be fired at a mysterious vessel seen entering the closed waters. The boat turned out to be an
innocent fisherman, but these may well have been the first shots fired in the Second World War.
The structure was eventually demobilised in the 1950s and sold at auction to private owners. It has
changed hands several times but is now owned by the Darroch family, who have opened it to the
public, offering a number of displays and exhibitions. After decades of declining popularity, there
are currently plans to give New Brighton a fresh lease of life, with the addition of a supermarket, a
new hotel, a cinema, bars, restaurants, and a water sports centre with a new model boating lake.

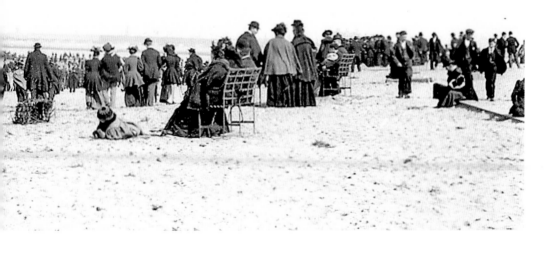

CENTRAL STATION

BIRKENHEAD'S CENTRAL STATION (below), as it was the 1930s. The year 1886 saw the creation of Mersey Railway, which, as the building proudly states, was the quickest route to Liverpool. Work had begun five years earlier and at its peak the project employed nearly 1,400 men. Initially progress was sluggish, with only small explosives and pick axes engaged in breaking through the earth. Later, a compressed air boring machine, the Beaumont Cutter, was put to work and successfully pushed the project much nearer to completion. When it opened, eight powerful steam locomotives running from Liverpool's James Street connected with Hamilton Square, running onto Birkenhead Central before concluding at Green Lane. This allowed speedy cross-river journeys at a fraction of the time it took on the ferries. On the first day alone, approximately 36,000 passengers climbed aboard the carriages to experience this new engineering marvel. Early commuters disliked the noise and soot of the journey but by the time this photograph was taken the line had been electrified, allowing a more pleasurable journey. Three taxicabs can be seen waiting outside the station as their drivers wait to pick up disembarking passengers; a policeman looks on from the middle of Borough Road.

BIRKENHEAD'S CENTRAL STATION is still very much in use on the Mersey rail network and is one of the more well-used stations in the town. This stop was once the nearest for commuters to

disembark for Birkenhead town centre, until the opening of the county's newest station in 1998, Conway Park. The old three-station network has expanded greatly to cope with consumer demand, with a number of new connections being made throughout the early 1900s. The 1970s saw the construction of a loop and link line connecting the city stations to the Cheshire Lines network and the Lancashire and Yorkshire tracks. There has also been a big increase in the number of trains on the tracks. There are now a total of fifty-nine trains in operation, transporting passengers above and beneath the bustling streets of Merseyside. This modern day photograph (above) shows where the original text can still be seen high upon the station's brickwork. However, with the Queensway tunnel to Liverpool only yards away, it is now arguable whether or not the railway is actually faster than road. The station itself has remained largely unchanged, although a number of chimneys have been removed, along with the passenger shelters of those earlier days.

GRANGE ROAD WEST

THIS EARLY TWENTIETH-century urban scene shows Grange Road West in Birkenhead town centre. The road has a similar origin to that of Grange Road (which can be seen in the distance) and is shown here busy with people. A young boy has taken a particular interest in the photographer as he stands a few yards ahead of the bakers William Singleton & Son's horse and cart. To his left a woman can be spotted peering from the doorway of a confectioner, which has advertisements for chocolate placed upon its windows. The shop next door is empty, but for a number of years was the daily workplace of Miss Jane Dow. She was a furrier who specialised in repairing and altering fur clothing for the more well-to-do ladies of the town. A few paces behind the cameraman stood the Grange Road West Drill Hall, used as the headquarters of the 1st Volunteer Battalion, Cheshire Regiment. They were commonly referred to as the Cheshire Greys, as was the colour of their uniform. One hundred and fifty members of the battalion risked their lives during the Boer War conflict of 1899-1902, four of whom fell in battle.

GRANGE ROAD WEST today is still one of the main streets in Birkenhead town centre, but the nature of the commercial properties in the area has changed considerably. The confectionery store and the adjoining property have been knocked through to make one large premises, currently in use as a café under the name of Cramstones. Next door is a clothing shop, Isha, which specialises in providing Indian-style garments for the women of the neighbourhood. On the corner of Eastbourne Road is the decorating store Paints 'R' Us. This was once the property of Louis Pollock, a perambulator manufacturer who sold an assortment of cradles and prams for Birkenhead babies. Protective awnings are no longer deemed necessary for today's modern establishments and neither are the old fashioned cobbles, which have been replaced with tarmac.

THE PRENTON HOTEL

THIS 1930S VIEW shows the Prenton Hotel situated on the corner of Borough Road and Prenton Road West. Like many parts of Wirral, this bit of the peninsula was once covered by acres of fertile fields and farmland. As local towns grew, residential developments slowly but surely encroached upon these unspoilt landscapes and, by the time this photograph was taken, Prenton sported a population of just over 2,000 residents. It was also in this decade that the Prenton Hotel first opened its doors. It had gained its alcohol licence from the Old Feathers public house, which was once situated in Chester Street, but demolished to make way for the Mersey tunnel approach roads. This new pub was ideally situated to draw in the crowds from the area's most successful football team, Tranmere Rovers. The club's ground, Prenton Park, is located right across the street to the left of this image. Previous to this, the ground had been located on the other side of the road, but in 1912 the club moved to the opposite land on Borough Road to a brand new stadium. It had stands

on both sides of the pitch, a paddock and three open terraces with a total capacity of almost 17,000.

THE PRENTON HOTEL remains a favourite haunt for many local drinkers and on match days this pub certainly becomes crowded! It changed its name to the Prenton Park Hotel during the mid-twentieth century to reflect its close ties with the nearby football stadium, but nowadays it is simply known as the Prenton Park. The building has remained largely unaltered in its eighty-year history and, on looking closely, the original signs above the doors for the lounge and the games room can still be seen. Tranmere Rovers Football Club remains Wirral's most prominent team and they continue to play at their adored home ground, Prenton Park. The player Dixie Dean is usually recognised as Rovers' most famous son. Born in Laird Street in 1907, Dean's unrivalled skills on the pitch gained him the respect of football fans nationwide. He scored twenty-seven goals in twenty-seven matches for Rovers in the 1924/5 season and Everton FC soon snapped him up. In 1927 Dean was selected to play for England and remained in the squad for five years. He is remembered by teams on both sides of the Mersey and has gained an almost legendary status with modern day supporters. His record of an amazing sixty goals in a single season still stands today.

BIRKENHEAD PARK
ENTRANCE

THIS TWENTIETH-CENTURY view depicts a blustery day beneath the grand entrance to Birkenhead Park. The idea for a public park came from Liverpool shipping magnet and town commissioner Sir William Jackson. With the remarkable skill of design genius Joseph Paxton, work commenced to transform an area of unhealthy swampland into a blossoming Victorian paradise. In 1847 the project was finally complete. This was to be the first ever official public park in the world with over 100 acres of landscaped gardens, lakes and pathways made available for all. The colossal renovation took over 1,000 men more than three years to complete, at a cost of approximately £70,000. Here we see the main entrance on the corner of Park Road North and Park Road East. The gatehouse was designed by James Gillespie Graham, the mastermind behind Hamilton Square. Inside, it contains two lodges on either side known as the North and South

Lodges; these add to the very imperial look of this inner-city section of Wirral. At the time, this impressive gateway allowed Birkenhead to vie with such famous architectural wonders as London's Marble Arch and the iconic Arc De Triomphe in Paris.

ON VISITING BIRKENHEAD Park today you will notice that the imposing and robust stone gatehouse continues to stand with a truly awesome visual impact. The central archway stands at 43ft high and draws the eye through to the gardens within. All of the original stone columns have survived and have been superbly maintained over the years. They provide a somewhat Roman influence to this northern shipping town. Looking up, the date mark of 1847 can be spotted inscribed upon the top centre of the structure. The park was opened on 5 April of that year; this day was chosen to coincide with the opening of the Birkenhead dock system. On that date, the surviving cobbles seen in the foreground of this image were trod by masses of people, no less than 56,000, who had turned out to celebrate this milestone. The park became an international sensation and left a great impression on one American visitor, Frederick Olmsted. He came to Birkenhead twice in the 1850s; from it he drew inspiration for the design of his own public project, the now world-famous Central Park in New York City.

NEW CHESTER ROAD

NEW FERRY'S NEW Chester Road in the 1930s. This road was built in the mid-1800s to create a faster travelling route, bypassing the villages of Wirral, to Chester. The previous highway was then renamed the Old Chester Road. The new rapid thoroughfare came with a price; this section of road once housed a toll bar. Drivers wishing to use this route would have to pay a small fee, or otherwise take the longer and more winding routes through Higher and Lower Bebington. The toll remained in place until 1883. This much later view looking up towards Rock Ferry shows a busy afternoon street scene. A branch of the Westminster Bank is located to the left and dates from the early 1900s. It once provided financial services to local workers, a number of whom can be seen making their way about town. In the middle of the road a police officer, attired in a

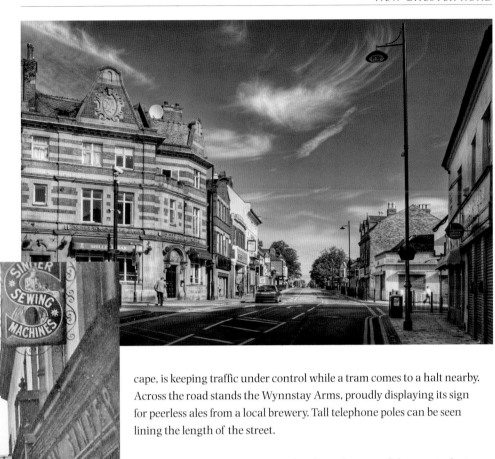

cape, is keeping traffic under control while a tram comes to a halt nearby. Across the road stands the Wynnstay Arms, proudly displaying its sign for peerless ales from a local brewery. Tall telephone poles can be seen lining the length of the street.

OBSERVING NEW CHESTER Road in the early years of the twenty-first century, some remarkable similarities are revealed. The road itself had remained a main route in and out of Wirral and can be found heaving with commuting traffic on most weekdays. The former Westminster Bank is now known as the Shillings Bar and is located at the junction of the pedestrianised Bebington Road. Other such pubs exist in this part of New Ferry, including Alice's Bar and the historic Farmer's Arms; the Wynnstay Arms, however, is no more. Simple Credit, a cheque-cashing and currency exchange centre, now occupies the corner premises. To the extreme right there was once a small shop selling a variety of Singer sewing machines; these were some of the most popular products of the nineteenth and early twentieth century. With advances in domestic technology, the demand for such items has dropped dramatically and now the old sewing store is part of the Citizens Advice Bureau. The dated telephone poles have also disappeared and now the road is lined with streetlights. A policeman is a rare sight on New Chester Road nowadays; instead a security camera now scans the vicinity.

CHRIST CHURCH

PORT SUNLIGHT'S DIVINE example of religious architecture stands in the appropriately named Church Drive in the centre of the village. It was opened on 8 June 1904 at the expense of the ever-benevolent William Hesketh Lever. He had approached the Warrington design firm William & Segar Owen, who drew up plans for a wonderful new place of worship for the whole village to enjoy. With the blueprints in hand, Lever ordered men from his own building department, within the Lever Brothers' factory, to begin construction. The church is made from fine red sandstone taken from a Helsby quarry and covered with a stone slated roof. The square tower is home to eight bells, the heaviest of which weighs nearly three quarters of a ton. Lever was a man of quality and, as such, employed the services of Henry Willis & Sons, a firm recognised to be one of the best organ manufactures of the time. It was to be the largest musical organ in the whole of Wirral and was

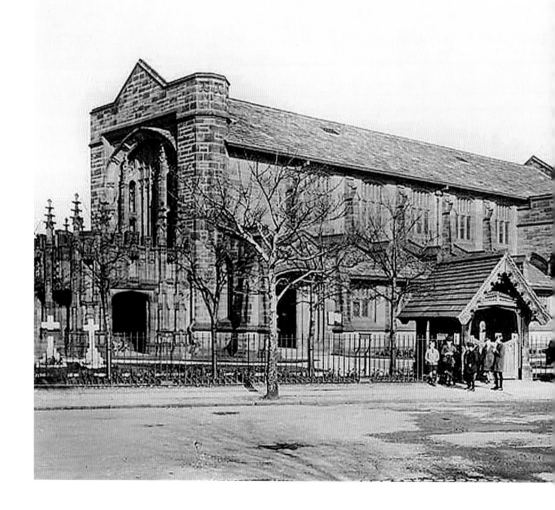

regularly played to the 800 parishioners who congregated for holy worship each and every Sunday. This image dates from the 1930s and shows several children standing at the ornamental lychgate of the church.

THIS SACRED BUILDING has survived two world wars and appears unscathed and almost identical to how it looked when it was consecrated just over a hundred years ago. It is famous locally for its array of beautiful stained-glass windows, each representing an aspect of church life since the time of the reformation. Outside in the narthex, to the left of the image, stands the tomb of the first Viscount Leverhulme and his wife, Lady Lever. She passed away in 1913; the Lady Lever Art Gallery was named in her honour. Lord Lever (by then Lord Leverhulme) succumbed to pneumonia in 1925. On 11 May of that year, Christ Church swelled to capacity as it was descended upon by immense numbers of mourners, who gathered together to pay their final respects to the late Lord Leverhulme, who would be greatly missed. Christ Church is now part of the wider United Reformed Church, which came about from the collaboration of the Presbyterian Church of England, the Congregational Church in England and Wales, the Re-formed Association of Churches of Christ and the Congregational Union of Scotland. Services at Christ Church are held every Sunday morning and afternoon, with separate communions and baptisms at various times throughout the month. It is one of the most well visited attractions in Port Sunlight.

DERBY BATHS

HERE WE SEE the well-attended Derby Baths in the year 1933. The 1930s saw Wirral Council build a number of public pools, including a second in this area further down by the funfair and another, revived and refurbished, in Hoylake. This photograph was taken just a year after the baths were officially opened by its namesake, Lord Derby, at Harrison Drive in Wallasey. The pool was built at a cost of £35,000; it was open air, with enough space to allow 1,000 bathers to take a dip in the often chilly waters. Being 100 yards long by 25 yards wide and 7ft deep, the pool could often be found full of swimmers and spectators, especially on a hot summer's day. It also had enough roof space for 200 scantily clad sunbathers. The pool was very close to one of Wallasey's beaches, known as Mockbeggar Bay. Legend has it that this coastal treasure was named after Mockbeggar Hall, now otherwise known as Leasowe Castle, situated further down the shoreline. In the background are a number of golden sand dunes, which provided many a youngster a fun

place to run about and play. They also doubled as a marvellous place to sit and take in the undisturbed views across the scenic Liverpool Bay.

A COMPLETE TRANSFORMATION has taken place; this part of Wallasey and its historic swimming pool have now been replaced by a pub and restaurant. The Derby Pool is part of the nationwide Harvester chain and now stands in Bay View Drive. This new building was only completed in the late 1990s, in a fashionable but distinctly older Art Deco style. It stands slightly adjacent to the old site of the swimming pool, which is now covered by a vast area of green grassy lawns, creating a peaceful and quiet refuge for a meal and a drink. Many patrons enjoy watching the sun set over the bay from the outdoor seating area; it is only one of few such establishments left operating in the area. The Derby Pool has a great family atmosphere and is open for business every day between the hours of 11 a.m. and 11 p.m. Twenty-first-century renaissance development company, Neptune, are planning to include a brand new open-air swimming pool in the heart of Wallasey, as part of their multimillion pound master plan for the town. If all is successful, Wallasey shall once again have a fantastic public pool to attract the masses.

CONWAY STREET

TO THE RIGHT of this image, taken in 1912, stands an ornate tram trolley pole with its electric wires stretching high above the people below. It stands complete with lanterns, lit at night to help guide the driver's way. John Woolman & Son's Printers & Stationers is situated at the corner of Bank Street to the left of the shot, with the edge of a motor car dealership just in view. Next door, proudly flying a flag from a second storey window, is the shop of Mr Oxton, a clothier and outfitter. Continuing along this row of stores there is a second tailor shop and a furniture dealer under the name of Black & Sons. A customer or employee from the latter appears to have noticed the photographer as he peers out from the shop doorway. Looking ahead, as the road merges

with Argyle Street, is the confectionary store of Charles Stanley. His window display advertises a tempting stock of chocolate to those in Birkenhead possessing a sweet tooth.

THIS PART OF Conway Street has been transformed by the construction of the Mersey tunnel, with many of the buildings of the past being completely removed without a trace. The street is considerably shorter now as the tunnel approach road makes up part of this old busy thoroughfare. To the left we see the corner of the old car dealership. This building spent many years operating as a cinema, before closing down in the 1990s. In recent years the site has become something of a financial challenge for various nightclub owners; it is currently unoccupied. Over the road from Bank Street Sherlock's Bar now operates. It encompasses both the former stationary premises and outfitter's building, making one large club. Next door, with its blue and green neon sign, is Mario's, a takeaway offering pizza, burgers and kebabs to revellers after a night out. In the distance, clad with grey panelling, is the side of St Mark's House, which houses a number of legal companies including the Crown Prosecution Service.

YMCA BUILDING

THE PHOTOGRAPH OPPOSITE of Grange Road shows the Birkenhead branch of the Young Men's Christian Association. This grand building, with its classical arched entrance, was opened in 1890 at a cost of £9,000, but despite being the headquarters of the town's YMCA, its most famous associations are with the Boy Scout Movement. In 1906 Baden-Powell visited the town to give a speech about the role of military scouting and youth culture. He returned in 1908 with a new speech and a new idea. On that occasion he publicly inaugurated the Boy Scout Movement, starting a scheme that would be adopted by boys all over the world. The very first scout group was formed in Birkenhead soon after, as was the very first scout hut, which was built at the corner of Borough Road and North Road. Next door, to the left, we can see the railings of the Grange Road Baptist Church. This was a large Parthenon-style structure with enough seating for 600 parishioners. Looking further up the road there is the big corner building of Daniel Evans & Co. They carried out a drapery and milliner service from their store at the junction of Catherine Street.

SADLY THE IMPRESSIVE arched doorway has been lost over the years and now a much simpler and plainer entrance guides shoppers into the clothing store Primark. The stylish brickwork still remains but the lower half of the building is now mostly made up of a glass frontage. After nearly fifty years of service, a lack of funding became a serious problem for the YMCA and, in 1935, they were forced to sell up to British Home Stores. The building has remained as retail premises ever since. The classical Baptist church is also no longer in existence, having been sold to a retail chain in the same decade. Woolworths moved from their store several yards down and built a brand new building on the former holy site in 1938. They traded there until the century-old firm went into administration. Looking up we can see that the former premises of Daniel Evan's drapery business is standing empty, but it is set to become the new location for an Asda store. When completed, officials predict that it will generate 320 new full and part-time jobs for the town, and help to breathe new life into the high street.

ST JAMES' CHURCH AND DOCK COTTAGES

THE CHURCH HAS an 'island' location and stands at the intersection of no less than seven distinct roads leading to and from the various districts of Wirral. This shot was taken in 1913, by which time the church had been there for fifty-five years and had held many religious sermons. St James' had been built in 1858 as a place of worship for the inhabitants of what were known as the Dock Cottages (or Queens Buildings), which can be seen in the background. They were arguably the earliest block of flats in England and, at four storeys high, they housed approximately 1,600 residents. The cottages were based upon what was known as the 'Scotch Plan', after similar tenement blocks were built in Edinburgh and Glasgow. Each room had clean running water, a convenient dust shaft, adequate ventilation and other sanitary necessities. On inspecting these new developments, one architectural critic described Birkenhead as 'the city of innovation', and early tenants favoured their new homes most highly. One Victorian mother attested to the

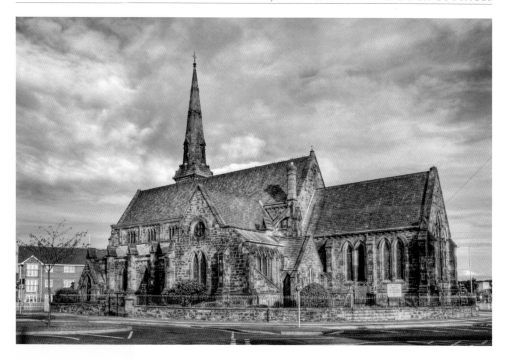

superior convenience of the layout and enjoyed the relief from weather exposure that was to be found in many working-class dwelling houses at the time.

THIS TWENTY-FIRST-century comparison shows little change to St James' Church and it still remains at its 'island' location, albeit often amongst much more traffic than during its earlier years. The building has survived largely unchanged since its construction and still provides a place of worship for residents of, what has become known as, the North End of the town. Additional altruistic developments have arisen from the church, with the Bidston & St James' Children's Centre situated nearby offering support and advice for young families in the area. There is also the St James' Neighbourhood College; it works with Wirral Metropolitan College to provide valuable education and training courses to all ages. The St James' Library also helps to provide education and learning to the people of Birkenhead and is situated only several yards from the church in Laird Street; it houses a large number of books and ICT facilities. The demolition of the old Dock Cottages took place in the late 1930s and a second estate of residential flats was built and christened Ilchester Square. These, however, lasted less than forty years and nowadays, modern flats and semi-detached houses occupy the location.

ST LAURENCE'S CHURCH

ST LAURENCE'S CHURCH stands here at the corner of Beckwith Street and Park Street in approximately 1900. The original building was constructed in 1866; Father Frederick Waterhouse took the first ecclesiastical post. He was ordained, along with two other new clergymen, by the Bishop of Shrewsbury in St Werburgh's Chapel in Grange Lane, in that same year. A second, more accommodating church was commissioned in the 1870s, but the construction of the Mersey railway underground tunnel a decade later resulted in some serious damage. Another rebuild of the church was ordered; this time it was to be more graceful in style, as depicted in the photograph. The image also displays the presbytery to the left of the shot. It was located next door to St Laurence's School, which was first set up in the mid-nineteenth century. A number of poorly-clothed and barefooted local children can be seen chatting in the street, as others stand coyly on the Beckwith Street pavement looking over with interest. This street was the site of Birkenhead's first reported murder way back in 1852; sailor William Green was found lying dead not far from this very scene.

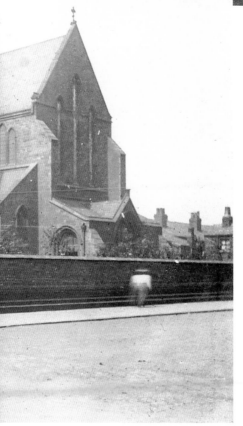

THIS PART OF the town is very different to how it was over a century ago. The church is now gone, having been demolished in the 1990s after a decline in attendance figures. Unassuming houses now stand in its place in the aptly named St Laurence Close. The vicinity's layout is also very different, as the actual junction of Beckwith Street and Park Street has also disappeared. The old St Laurence's School building was pulled down in the late 1960s and, until recently, local children attended its successor, which was based on the same site, now known as St Laurence Drive. In 2010, it was decided that falling pupil numbers have rendered the school unfeasible and town councillors have decided to close it. On hearing the news, one parent was reported to have said, 'over 100 years of history will be wiped out, just like St Laurence's Church.' It is predicted that most of the remaining children shall be relocated to St Werburgh's primary school in Park Grove to continue their education.

LADY LEVER ART GALLERY

AFTER LADY LEVER died from pneumonia in 1913, a devastated Lord Lever set about making plans to honour her memory. The following year, designs for a brand new art gallery had been finalised by William & Segar Owen and its construction was soon underway. King George V and Queen Mary laid down the foundation stone for the Lady Lever Art Gallery during a Royal visit to the village in March 1914; they did so using a remote control from Hulme Hall. It was built with Portland Stone clad over a body of reinforced concrete. Marble bases were included at each of the entrance steps and doors on the south of the building were flanked with stone urns. In 1930 the remarkable memorial obelisk, seen here in the centre of the photograph, was erected in honour of Lord Lever, who died five years previously. It was designed by his godson, James Lomax Simpson, and sculptured impeccably from bronze and granite by William Reid Dick. The figures at its base represent Industry, Education, Charity and Art. Inspiration stands

high on top. It was these traits that were thought to most successfully represent Lord Lever's long and tireless work for Port Sunlight.

THIS ELEGANT GALLERY has remained an impressive focal point of the village and many thousands of visitors come to Port Sunlight every year. It houses an amazing collection of eighteenth and nineteenth-century paintings, Georgian furniture and one of the country's greatest collections of Wedgewood pottery ever compiled. The gallery continues to showcase new and fascinating exhibitions from its vast collections and neighbouring establishments. One such example was the recent Old Master Drawings Exhibition. It featured work from a number of great Italian Renaissance and Northern European artists between 1500 and 1800 and proved very popular with the public. The gallery has recently added several new activity rooms, which, it is hoped, will encourage some of the younger members of Wirral society to engage with the creative world of art and sculpture. It is open daily from 10 a.m. to 5 p.m. with free admission to all.

OLD POST OFFICE HOTEL

OVER IN ARGYLE Street we see the Old Post Office Hotel. This building was certainly constructed by 1860, when it was known as the less aged Post Office Hotel in local directories. Two respectable looking gentlemen can be seen standing at the main door and a large advertisement of Yates' Ales is prominently perched high up in the centre of the three-storey building. Yates' brewery supplied alcohol to many establishments in Cheshire and Lancashire and had worked from a local brewery

yard in Market Place since the 1830s. This pub sits in between Conway Street and Oliver Street and would have been a popular drinking spot with the employees from many nearby establishments including the post office buildings, the Argyle Theatre and the Poor Law offices.

NOWADAYS THE OLD Post Office Hotel often functions as a dance studio. At the time this photograph was taken it had become High Society nightclub and before that it was Sophie's bar. This location has proved a difficult one for businesses to flourish in, especially in the current economic climate, which threatens the success of many of the town's drinking establishments. Nevertheless, the building's exterior appears to have been kept in excellent condition; the roof has been altered since the previous image was taken in 1910. Clearly visible is the Old Post Office Hotel name, which has been branded across one half of the building. The downstairs windows have also been altered and they now stand approximately 8ft high either side of the original brick portico. Upstairs, the two central windows and the upper-right window have all been improved and now allow much more light into the private areas of the property.

HOYLAKE RAILWAY STATION

HOYLAKE RAILWAY STATION is shown here in approximately 1905, nearly forty years after its completion. The station had been long awaited by the residents of the area and after several sittings of Parliament the Bill to build was finally passed. Captain Ritchie, a Government inspector, surveyed the new line and found it met official standards and declared the railway open to traffic in June 1866, and open to public trains the following month. The whole length of the line was to be seven miles long, running from Hoylake to the river, passing through Hoose (a nearby village), Meols, Moreton, Bidston and so on, all the way to Seacombe. However, parts of the track had not been finished in time, so early passengers were forced to finish their journey by way of omnibuses at Wallasey. These omnibuses were extremely busy and became so crowded that certain brave passengers even attempted to jump from the train as it was still pulling into the station so they could race to catch the bus! The creation of this new station had a great effect upon the population of Hoylake. Upon opening, its residents numbered nearly 2,000, but

by 1901 this had more than trebled. In this image we can see several of these inhabitants patiently waiting on the platform; a number of stalls and shops can be seen further along too.

THE STATION IS still in operation and is on the West Kirby branch of Mersey rail's Wirral Line. In 1938 the line was electrified and the steam engines of old done away with, as well as the aged Victorian station itself. A brand new Art Deco style building was commissioned in the modernistic 'London transport' style of Charles Holden and it was to be designed by the architects of the London, Midland and Scottish Railway. The prominent circular clerestory over the booking hall can be seen on the top left of this image. These days the station becomes particularly popular with the world's golfing community when the nearby Royal Liverpool Golf Club is chosen to host the Open Championship. Since 1897, Hoylake has hosted eleven such events, with the next Championship event due to take place here in 2014. In 2006 the station underwent a £600,000 refurbishment, including the replacement of the booking hall floors, the addition of an accessible ticket counter for disabled people and a complete redecoration inside and out.

GREENDALE ROAD, PORT SUNLIGHT

THESE SPLENDID COTTAGES stand in Port Sunlight's very scenic Greendale Road in the 1930s. They date from the year 1902 and were designed by the Liverpool firm of Talbot and Wilson. The cottages were purposely built to resemble Kenyon Peel Hall in Little Hulton (just south of Lord Lever's hometown of Bolton), which was once a large timber manor dating from Elizabethan times. These were just seven of the ninety-seven cottages that stood on this long road running parallel to the rail track; they were designed to give the best impression of Port Sunlight. Further down the road there stood the first ever village shop at the corner of Park Road, which opened in 1891. The road also became the location of the Lever Free Library & Museum when it was converted from the Girls' Hostel in 1903. Gladstone Hall, with dining and recreation rooms for the male workforce of Port Sunlight, was also built here. Prime Minister

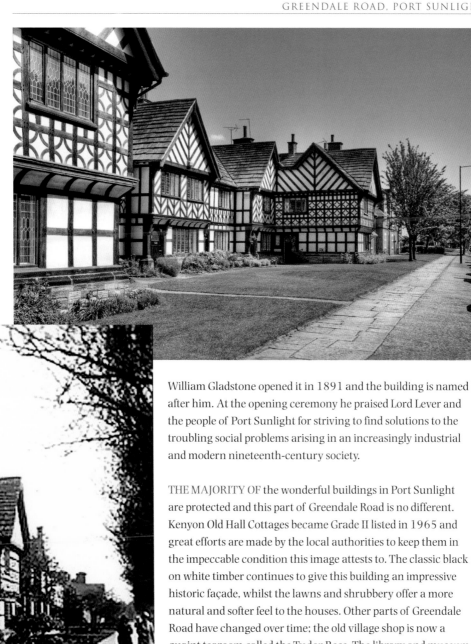

William Gladstone opened it in 1891 and the building is named after him. At the opening ceremony he praised Lord Lever and the people of Port Sunlight for striving to find solutions to the troubling social problems arising in an increasingly industrial and modern nineteenth-century society.

THE MAJORITY OF the wonderful buildings in Port Sunlight are protected and this part of Greendale Road is no different. Kenyon Old Hall Cottages became Grade II listed in 1965 and great efforts are made by the local authorities to keep them in the impeccable condition this image attests to. The classic black on white timber continues to give this building an impressive historic façade, whilst the lawns and shrubbery offer a more natural and softer feel to the houses. Other parts of Greendale Road have changed over time; the old village shop is now a quaint tearoom called the Tudor Rose. The library and museum building has since become the village Heritage Centre, which has a fascinating museum inside. Its mission is to collect, preserve and tell the stories behind the people, buildings and landscapes of Port Sunlight. Further along, at the end of Greendale Road, is Gladstone Hall; it is now known as the Gladstone Theatre though. It features a variety of different shows and concerts all year round, often to a jam-packed 500-seat auditorium.

VICTORIA ROAD, NEW BRIGHTON

NEW BRIGHTON'S VICTORIA Road, pictured here in 1902. This part of the resort was known locally as the Horseshoe; it was the terminus for trams where they would negotiate the curvy tracks and start their return journey. The building to the right was the Criterion Restaurant, which was first established in 1851. It was the oldest licensed restaurant in New Brighton and boasted splendid views of the river and the promenade. The large corner building was the Royal Ferry Hotel, run by Thomas Vowles. This was also opened in the 1850s and was conveniently situated to attract visitors from the ferry, which began operating the following decade. The pier was

approximately 730ft long and was built on strong iron pillars set into the shore.
Alongside stands a public promenade, which was constructed shortly afterwards
in September 1867. Hundreds of people attended its celebratory opening;
each person paid sixpence to gain access to the pier. It was a very substantial
structure at 550ft long and 130ft wide and was home to a number of popular
seaside cafés, saloons and entertainment facilities. From then on New Brighton's
popularity rocketed; it became the indisputable Victorian holiday paradise.

BY THE 1920S the pavilion's popularity was waning and it was closed down in
1923. The pier was reconstructed several years later after being purchased by
the Wallasey Corporation and it became a crowd-pulling success for many years.
Its fortunes faded in 1971 when it was decided that the ferry service should
cease to operate due to a huge decline in popularity and the ever-increasing
number of cars being used. This, in turn, had a catastrophic effect upon the
pavilion and it was finally demolished in 1978. In remarkable contrast, Victoria
Road, in the above image, bears little evidence of its former fame as the main
street of this once incredible seaside wonderland. The two piers have gone, as
has the 'horse shoe' tramlines that were once set into the road. Looking right,
the former Criterion Restaurant is now a pub called Redcaps, named after Old
Mother Redcap, a Wallasey woman renowned with assisting smugglers and
wreckers in the eighteenth century. The grand Royal Ferry Hotel went on to
become the Chelsea Reach nightclub in the 1980s, but nowadays the building is
used as residential apartments; it is known as the Chelsea Plaza.

Other titles published by The History Press

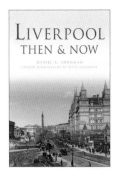

Liverpool Then & Now
DANIEL K. LONGMAN

Liverpool's rich heritage is uniquely reflected in this fascinating new compilation. Contrasting a selection of forty-five archive images alongside full-colour modern photographs, this book delves into the changing faces of Liverpool. Comparing the fashionable man about town to his modern counterparts, and featuring famous landmarks and little-known street scenes, this is a wide-ranging look at the city's colourful history that will provide present occupants with a glimpse of how the city used to be, in addition to awakening nostalgic memories for those who lived here in the past.

978 0 7524 5740 6

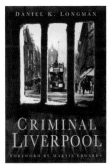

Criminal Liverpool
DANIEL K. LONGMAN

Criminal Liverpool is an entertaining and informative round-up of some of the strangest, most bloodthirsty and appalling crimes that took place in and around Liverpool from the Victorian era up to the mid-twentieth century. Daniel K. Longman's research digs deep and sheds new light on local *cause célèbres*. This readable text is supported by fascinating illustrations and will appeal to everyone who has an interest in the sinister aspects of the city's history.

978 0 7509 4749 7

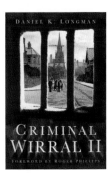

Criminal Wirral II
DANIEL K. LONGMAN

In this fascinating follow-up to *Criminal Wirral* you'll find intriguing cases of strange, despicable and comical crimes that have been long forgotten, accompanied by striking illustrations that bring these events to life. You'll discover the grisly facts about what once lay floating in Birkenhead Park pond and the gruesome details of a suicide on board a Woodside-bound locomotive. *Criminal Wirral II* will appeal to everyone who has an interest in the darker side of Wirral's history.

978 0 7524 5007 0

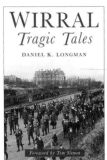

Wirral Tragic Tales
DANIEL K. LONGMAN

Daniel K. Longman looks at the accidents and disasters from across the Wirral from the mid-nineteenth century to the early twentieth century – in the countryside and in the towns, and in Birkenhead and Ellesmere Port's chemical factories. From the sad to the spectacular, from overdoses and omnibus crashes to the most incredible unintentional firework display, this book brings together a collection of stories to fascinate and enthrall all those who know the Wirral peninsula.

978 0 7509 4674 2

Visit our website and discover thousands of other History Press books.
www.thehistorypress.co.uk